Priscilla's Smile

By Josephine J. Bridgers

Priscilla's Smile

By Josephine J. Bridgers

copyright 2011

All Rights Reserved. No part of this book should be transmitted or reproduced by means of: electronic, mechanic, this includes photocopying, recording or any information storage and retrieval system without the permission from the copyright owner,

Josephine Jenkins Bridgers

(Book Cover design for Priscilla's Smile Two by Denise Sharpe)

Artist: Reginald A. Bridges contact no. 252-885-3836

Rbridgesjr1978@gmail.com

Imprint: Jan'na HCS

Bio: The author's niece, Priscilla Jenkins

Priscilla Jenkins was so spirited and filled with aspirations. She was a people person; she never met a stranger. At an early age, she pushed for a better life. She became a beautician and devoted her life to improving women and men's appearance. She also loved to decorate and did floral arrangements. She worked two jobs. Along with working as a Beautician, she worked as a lead worker at QVC and she became well known as the young woman with rising potential while she continued to establish a good work history. Priscilla prided herself in doing the best; she listened to her customers and when they left her beauty salon, they looked like a million bucks. All her energy was poured in her work, but when she became sick, she became powerless. Her spirit remained positive despite her illness. She loved life that's why the author symbolized butterflies in memory of her beautiful niece. We got closer on the end of her journey. She talked about making a special dinner for the author even in her delicate state. **I looked at my niece affectionately, telling her I loved her and then Priscilla Smiled.** Several days later, this beautiful precious spirit was gone!

Introduction

Priscillia's Smile Two is a revision of Priscilla's Smile and Memento, but with a soulful twist of words while the author takes you on a journey that will leave you speechless. Priscilla's Smile Two is a collection of poems selected to speak to the audience in a way that words can' t articulate.

These poets in this collection walk you on a expedition using their imaginations and their experiences. This book represents different genres, but has a common goal which is to excite your critical thinking. Whether you are experiencing joy or sadness, Priscilla' s Smile Two will plant a smile on your face. The author's guide is movtivated by these themes:

A Time to Live, a Time to be Happy, a Time to be Sad and a Time to Love.

This book takes you on a pleasurable escapade and the author hopes that you can revisit your thoughts to a place where positive thinking rekindles joy. Priscilla's Smile Two is a motivational piece for those yearning to be heard but can't articulate their own words.

The author enlisted family members for this book to complete her vision. The author believes that life holds many treasures and believes that if we stand on its foundation, we will cultivate our gift by watering it vocally or by written words. Sometimes in life we hold on to things that are less important instead of supporting each other when a friend is needed, or a listening ear is required.

Table of Content

When I close my eyes ……………............13
Wedding day Bliss…………………..........14-15
Success Means more than Riches…………………………...........16-18
In you I see Me……………………..........19-20
The Child's Needs…………………..........22-23
My Real Home…………………..........24-25
Getting Old……………………………...................26
A love that couldn't Speak …………………………………….............27-28
My Darling Black Rose……………….................................29-30
Love Don't Pay the Bills………….............31-33
Potrait of Love……………………………..35-36
On the Wings of an angel……………........38
Celebrating my daughter Birthday……………………………...........39-40
Timely Love………………...................41-42
Sweet Lullabye…………...................43-44
Fatherless………………………................45
The Little Lost Girl……………...........46-47
The unopened Present…………….............48
You don't Love Me………………............49-50
Invincible…………………………..............51
Grown Folk Love……………...........52-55
Pressing On……………..........................56
Time…………………………………..........58-59
No Regrets……………………….............61-62
Change……………………………............62
I am a man …………….........................63-64
Sucessful Failure………………….............65

Mr. Freeze..................................66
See the Light...........................67
Black Man 68
Fragment..................................69
Repercussions........................71
In the Midst of the
Darknes..............................72-73
Being in Love....................75-76
Heir..78
I Remembered...................79-80
Ghetto Language....................81
Power to do.......................82-83
Essence of
Fear..84
Helpless...................................85
Who Are You..........................86
Priceless Memories.................87
What Counts...........................88
I'll be There.............................89
True Lies..................................90
Senseless..................................91
Probably..................................92
Taste and See...........................92
Progress Onward....................94
Love Found.............................95
Respect....................................96

Through the eyes of a Warrior..97-98
Being a Man...99
Web of Lies...................................100-101
Wisdom..102
To know..103-106
No Cure..107-108
The Road to Riches.................109-110
Wasted Years............................111-112
Upbringing................................113-115
One way..116
Sins of this World....................117-118
You and They.......................................119
Me against Me..........................120-121
Lone Wolf...123
Real..124
Me and You, you and Me..125-129
Lovers of the Flesh..130
A Mother Pleads to her Son..131-132
To Live in Peace..................................133
Love doesn't happen by Chance..134
What does the Word Friend Means?..135-137

Africa We Hear Your Cry.................138-139
I live my story..............................140-141
Insight page..
Paying My Dues.........................143-146
An Angel in Waiting.................147-150
No Regrets......................................151
The Game Changing.....................152
Envisioning Rosa
Parks...153-154
Rosa Park, the bus.............................154-157

Friends..158-160
Think Positive..................................162
Feeling...................................163-164
Guard Your Heart........................165
The Reflection of My
Family...167-168
Dear Mom.......................................169
Letter to Mother........................171-172
Resistance...172
I walk alone....................................173-175
Let's get Acquainted..........................176-182
Potentail for greatness.......................183-185
Your Breath...186-188
Why should I care..............................189-190
That Child..191-192
Blood to Blood....................................193-194

We must make a moral effort to help empower others

It's the simple things that bring joy

When I close my eyes by JJB

When I close my eyes, I see light; a light that shines through the spirit of destitution. When I close my eyes, I see challenges; challenges that I have yet to overcome. When I close my eyes, I see honor; honor that has long been comprised by the simple everyday person. When I close my eyes, I dream; I dream of a milky white sky filled with watermelons hanging on the rim of the stars, angled sideways, as the rainbow of colored birds nest on the drops flowing from the dew of the clouds. But suddenly, when I open my eys, I see all the blessings life has to offer. A new day and a new tomorrow await. It's a pleasure to be alive.

Wedding Day Bliss by Josephine J. Bridgers

He touched me but I unhurriedly looked away. His eyes scanned over my imperfections with a yearning desire. He captivated me with his smile, as we stood wordless in the rain. He signaled for me to come closer while his eyes penetrated my soul. He exhausted my thoughts as I reflected back to the intimate moments we shared. We laughed while we carelessly threw rocks in the raging river. Instead of two silhouette images, our thoughts combined as one. We welcomed the midnight bliss. We emerged from the blistering heat, calm, due to the soothing rainfall. Consumed with our own preoccupation, we talked. Such a detail gesture but never less it was a definding moment when his lips touched mines. He moaned as if he was transformed into the mighty man of steel. This was our time, as two separate identities combine to form one union. Two beings unwinding to create one nucleus separated only by the wind.

Success means more than Riches or Fame by JJB

He is rich; he is poor.

How do you measure success?

Throwing titles here and there, does it really matter? He has a new car; he has a new house. Is your life complete?

Sit down and think! Do you feel a sense of relief? Do the things you treasure dearly give you an ounce of pleasure? Does anyone around you secretly or honestly really care? Everyone seems to think money is the key, but sit down and have a reality check, what really matters? Are the rich and famous happy or are they always in a state of beware? Everyone gives you praise when you are on cloud nine but as soon as you fall, where are the people you once knew? The answer to that question is, they are long gone. Stop! Look at things in a different perspective. Success means more than money, riches, or fame. Life requires endless struggles, yet the pain is deep, there will be nights when you go without any sleep. In your vulnerable state there will be times of quietness you might have to weep. But being able to show beauty within, that's what makes a person unique. Success isn't measured in monetary value because valuables last only for a while. Success is measured when you see the smiles when you approach people, now tell me, isn't it worthwhile? So, when someone approaches you and ask you, what do you do? Just tell them you are a successful person because you have people who care and love you.

In you I see me by Josephine J. Bridgers

In you, they see a bald head, and eyes with bags. In me, they see, a flat rear end and a thinning hairline. But what I see in you, I see a handsome man. Bags maybe, but filled with presents of little what nots from years of loving me. But in me they see thicknesss, bulges overpower my hips, "you can pinch more than a inch." My hair, you see a silver lining filled with years of you loving me and me loving you. Even though the world see a mortal man, I see a prince and I'm his princess. On our first romantic vacation, I watched from the window as he walked proudly back up the stairs, seeing me staring out the window his eyes ignited a sparkle while his love displayed his beautiful pearly whites in his alluring smile. It was just like the first time we met. Eyes blinded by beauty, the day time recaptured our youth and there glazing back in the mirror, two youthful beauties stood. No bags, hair glossy, and to our amazement, rejuvenated behinds! Through the years, we've grown into each other's skin. In him, I see me, a timeless love that has shattered the hourglass of time.

The Child's Need by Josephine J. Bridgers

Cuddled in a prone position there sits a young child. The child may be young but the burden of this world has already impacted her way of thinking. This young child has no one to love her, protect her innocence and most importantly, teach her to value her worth. This child's life has just begun, yet she has seen more than one child could ever hope to see or conquer in a lifetime. The child's eyes sparks as she sees a young couple pass by. The couple looks at every mole as they write down notes as if they were appraising a piece of furniture. But wait, the young couple retraced their steps, as they both question every detail of the young child's existence. Suddenly, for no apparent reason, they stopped. She wonders if there's hope at last. Will she have her own bed, decorated in a flower print with roses in the background, with hundreds of pink, brown, and yellow teddy bears decorating her own room while she relaxed for the night.

Will her night hold happy memories with a mommy and daddy singing her sweet songs at night? Will her night hold happy thoughts instead of hopeless regrets? It depended on this young couple. Did they want a boy or a girl? It depended on her smile, was it enough to captivate them, and will it change her entire world? Every young child has needs. The love that some take for granted, it only take just an ounce to make me please. I need a stable life filled of beautiful dreams so the hollow hole that creeps in my dreams at night will be blinded by the light, and the light will produce beautiful butterflies welcoming me to come and play. While I listened to beautiful music, my mind danced at the thought of just being loved. I hope this couple see from the mirror of my eyes. I am the one for them; the one that will cherish their love.

My Real Home by Josephine J. Bridgers

Yes, it's me, I got adopted by that couple that retraced their steps. I have a real home. A loving mother and a dutiful father. They couldn't take their eyes off me; they said my big brown eyes captured their attention causing them to retrace their steps.

I now have a little room covered with my favorite teddy bears, yellow, green, brown, pink, red and white. It's not fancy, but to a child, it priceless. My walls are painted with beautiful rivers flowing from end to end. It's the basic gift that nutures all my needs. Now, I truly have my own home. I hugged my pillow; this is what every child needs. A child longs for a stable home surrounded by loving parents. Parents that will nuture them and accept them as inquisitive beings. How could anyone not love me? I have two ponytails, a stunning smile, white teeth and skin that has a radiant shine. I am just a little child. I'm not vain. All I wanted was a simple home filled with tons of love. Parents that would look at me through the lens of love; that's all I ever wanted.

Getting Old by Josephine J. Bridgers

Here I am, a shadow blowing in the wind. My backbone is traumatized but my spirit elevates me high up in the trees next to a robin's nest. Tomorrow demolished. I see reflections of animals playing in the forest. The fall leaves evoke a warm feeling, but I am burdened down like the tar on the pavement. Endless love paused, while moments of pleasure devours any negative connotations. I paused. As time wonders around and around. Only dreams remain penetrating the hourglass while I sits patiently and wait to be called home because I am tired.

.A love that couldn't speak by JJB

Exquisite daisies draped in pinstriped ribbons, they symbolize romance fashioned to the scent of a flowery breeze. The flesh scent from the flowery buds arouse my senses. Why is going the distance so unbearable to the unwise? Have the dust encased my chest into a mountainous plains? The scent from the diced melons and cherries that I prepared the night before, oh my, they satisfied my taste buds. I pondered as I sat scrutinizing the flowers as they saluted their buds in the hot, humid summer heat. I remembered not long ago when snow and ice teased my lips for only a second prompting me to smile. But my thoughts were interrupted when I unexpectedtly saw a dog wobbling along with a squirrel. These picturesque bubbles of love, ride on the notes of songs. Notes that elevate me high in the clouds.

Unspoiled, these timeless moments when the rhythm of my chest is rejuvenated by the sting of a bumble bee. Then, on a misty blue day, my forgotten love shows his face. His body invokes his power over me. Hidden by the wrinkles embedded in my face from years of broken dreams. Slowly, slowly, he turns exposing his tears. Tears I welcomed like a friend. Then he reached out with his outstretched hands. His eyes told the love story that his voice couldn't tell.

"I love you," he whispered.

My Darling Black Rose by Matthew Jenkins Jr.

O how fragile your petals, green stalk

burdened with thorns. How unfortunate your

beauty, for it goes untouched, my darling

Black Rose. Please see what I see. Your worth

and beauty resonate exponentially for those

blessed to be in your presence. Succulent, Sweet Sad Black Rose. Allow time to melt away the painful reminiscence of thorns so sharp they pierce your supple skin and extend beyond your deepest self; schemingly placed so that not only are you protected, but your present yourself as a threat to the very word love. Please be healed, my Black Rose. O how fragile your petals, green stalk burdened with thorns. How fortunate for your beauty, for it goes untouched, for no one knows the pain that resides within you. Allow the warm light of love to help you grow for the special day you are embraced, My Black Rose

Love don't pay the bill by JJB

Poppy tails and centerpieces

I'm in love with my boo

He's my spirit when I sleep

The nucleus of every word I speak

Sunrise,

Sunset,

Hugging and kissing,

He's my sweet spirit of the streets

I'm too pretty to lift a broom

Nah, no books or education will suit my needs

Love is the main element of my hopes and dreams

You think I s'pose to work when I got my boo

Boom! The bubble burst (loud noise heard)

Giggling and laughing she suddenly stops

I'm having a baby, what am I to do?

I'm just a child

No job

No education

My boo is gone!

Invisible man is he

Fragrance of loveliness

consumes the air

Skyscraping the sky with vanilla

 wafers as pies

Little tales of dreams he told me

Butterflies

Cotton candy

Tales only one could dream

Looking down, the reality serves

as a wake-up call

A new life grows inside of me

Where is my boo now?

Then I remembered

What my momma said, "Child,

Love Don't Pay the Bills!"

**Why speak when the truth is
not
A priority**

Portrait of Love by JJB

Love is intangible, it's something that can't be touched, but it can be felt. Love has no fragrance, but what makes it unique is, it's a symphony that can't be heard but most definitely felt. If love doesnt hurt, why are so many sad? Is it because it invokes an indescribable feeling that can neither be expressed with tears or pearls? Love is tremendous. Even though some people think it can be bought, love brings out the beauty designed perfectly like gems. But for others, love is a prey of thought, the predator or the prey, it depends on the person seeking to retrieve it. For the selfish ones, they embrace it with empty words. Causing heartaches, an indescribable feeling that evokes many to cry. But few will ever obtain this luxury, because this adjective stands alone. It taunt people to pursue it while others just run away just to avoid the game hidden behind the thorns. But if you look closer, it is within your reach. But I view love as a portrait, it's invisible like a windstorm that gathers its strength from the blows of the dirt. Love has a taste of uncertainity. And yet for me, it is a mastering task just like a portrait encased in a frame not

meant to be claimed.

On the Wings of an Angel written by Brittany A. Hill

Though your tears may flow

As you experience

A pain no one can ever know

Take the time to cherish the memories and let love ease your mind. Embrace the footsteps of this ended legacy and come to know your identity, fulfill your purpose. And live in love, relieve your heavy heart. And rejoice in the start of her heaven sent rewards. As she rejoices among angels, may your tears cease and you no longer wail.

Be uplifted and remember

She's on the wings of an angel

Celebrating my daughter Birthday
written by Jamey Wilkins

Almost missed it

How could I?

Shocked

As I looked

Into the face of my watch, 5-26

All other thoughts

All other things

Immediately

Ceased to exist

A smile

A tear

Another year

Another month

Another minute

Of her life

Has passed

Without me in it

No letter

No Card

No call

She received

Nothing

That acknowledges

What she achieved

Wishes ungranted

Dreams shattered

Does it matter?

Nope because she

Won't get. a thing from me still....

I remembered

A timely love written by Jamey Wilkins

Yesterday ended when today began

Tomorrow comes when today ends

Time started as soon as I was born

Forever seemed so far away

Eternity will start as soon as I'm gone. And

tomorrow will always be today. Yesterday I

fell in love with you. And tomorrow I will still

because today I made a vow to love you until

eternity. Forever is not long enough

Cause it ends as soon as I die

So until forever comes, I want only you in my

life. You meant the world to me yesterday

But today you mean much more

By the time tomorrow comes, I will love you

even more than before I promise this through

eternity cause the only way I will depart, is when the day comes, you decide to break my heart.

Don't ever leave me!

Sweet Lullaby Take me Home
written by JJB

When I get old and my hair turns grey, look at all the wisdom that lies beneath each hair root. When my body seems to ache with every twist and turn. Don't hurry me away! My bones are brittle, my joints are stiff. When I sit nodding in my chair, recite a verse in the Bible, to let me know you still care. When the cataracts cause my eyes to become blurry, dim the lights, so I can dream of a life filled with colors with dainty flowers everywhere.
When my legs get flimsy and I can't make it up the stairs, be the shoulder that I can lean on, be the knight in my corner, the shield behind the glass. When the darkness covers my sight, pat me on the head, my dear child to

let me know everything is alright. When I lie down and breathe my last breath, don't be sad. I'm happy; there is no more pain. Don't cry any more tears. Sweet lullaby, sweet lullaby, take me home

COM' here my beloved daughter, sing me a sweet lullaby. So I can skip, hop, I'm finally going home.

Fatherless written by Jamey Wilkins

As I sit and watch how others play

I wonder if I would be different

Would I be the same, would I see the same

If my father wasn't missing

Would his presence inspire me

Would he guide me, mold me, and school me

Would I be better off or would I be worse

What if he beat and abused me

What if he drank all day? Then cursed me out

at night. Would I have followed his steps?

And been an alcoholic the rest of my life?

Maybe I'm better without one. Still, if I had

one, I wouldn't let him go. Cause maybe he'd

simply love me. But I didn't have a father so

I'll never know

The Little Lost Girl by JJB

The time is not known

The hours are not yet born

The someplace is hidden from a child

cuddling a warm blanket.

Why is the life of a child limited to a person's

imagination? Then, out of shame and fear, the

little lost child speaks, she says

"I am only one, but to a child of few I am a

little lost girl." Then she thinks out loud.

I am not defiant in the early stages of my life

Why are my instincts restricted to only my

mother's face? I am but one, a child, little but

lost. A child in a quest for the embracement

of her mother's arms. A child that will never

see the wrinkles in her father's face or hear

the loudness of his voice. But after all I am a

little lost girl. I have no ponytails, only a single braid, silky and black that rests down my small narrow head. My sisters and brothers are asleep but thoughts of playing are interrupted by the sounds erupting from my mother's room. I am quiet, as I escape to a pleasurable time, where there are no interruptions, no delays but where a little lost girl. Can go. Can laugh. Can be relax. Where a child has a momma, papa and siblings; she longed for structure. A place that has the highest regards for life and love."As she sits in the corner, quietly, she falls asleep

The Unopened Present written by Jamey Wilkins

All I ever wanted was to make momma proud That's all. And my purpose in life would be fulfilled. But the task has proven harder than expected. Where I thought I was strong, my weaknesses were revealed. Intentions were the best. So inside, I am at peace. Irregardless of what is depicted by the outer.

I tried, but I failed

So my words went unheard

Because my actions always seemed to speak louder

You don't Love me written by Brittany Anjanet Hill

I'm afraid to love you because you might hurt me. I'm afraid to hate you because I need you

Confused by my emotions

Misled by your fake devotion

What did I do so wrong for you to hate me?

In a sense, you took away my identity by denying your responsibility.

Time and time again, you let me down by never even coming around.

All my life I've wanted your love. You've denied me endless times.

Your unconditional love, I still can't find. My tears are falling because

I can't hate you. How can I love you inspite of everything u do?

Now I'm stronger, and I've taken away your power. Because from you, I reclaimed my identity

Invincible written by Jamey Wilkins

I don't know defeat, and chances are we will never meet.

My enemies cheat; because that is the only way they can compete.

I've got goals and with God's guide they will be completed.

I want to help those who have been denied and mistreated.

I look for loyalty in all that I know,

A friend is a friend, a foe is a foe. Stay close to the strong, and outgrow the weak.

I know right, I know wrong, but I don't know Defeat!

Grown Folk Love written by Jamey Wilkins

Sun kissed

Tan, Brown, Ebony, Bronze

In my arms forever

Is where you belong

Eyes like bottomless pits

So deep

Skin chocolatey rich

So sweet

My hand in your hand

Your hand in mine

Skipping along barefoot

Through the sands of time

Chasing the fading sun

Until we are deceased

Knowing you made it safely

Is the only way I'll rest in peace

When I placed you before me

I knew what it was

More than just infatuation

This is Grown Folk Love

Sun kissed

Bronze, Tan, Brown, Ebony

Only God can create

A bond so heavenly

Your hair

though not the longest

Is still without a doubt

The strongest

Your rib is my rib

My rib is yours

In you I found peace

After so many wars

Your touch alone

Can ease my storms

Whether a peck on the cheek

Or just a squeeze on my arm

Ever since that first time

I knew what it was

This aint no play-play stuff

Naw, this Grown Folks Love

Sun kissed

Ebony, Bronze, Tan, Brown

A smile creases my face

Whenever you come' round

A blessing

Our connection

Is a reflection

Of perfection

I'm your Adam

You're my Eve

On cruise control

You're my speed

No mile

Can separate us

No trial,can deflate us

You are joy to the Nth degree

I can't explain what you've meant to me. As

soon as you accepted me

I knew what it was

Not lust not a crush

Naw, this is Grown Folks Love

Sun kissed Ebony, Bronze, Tan, Brown

Pressing on written by JJB

The end of our journey is far within the cave. Why haven't this new generation paved the road for a new tomorrow? Have the beasts from the future enslaved our minds? Has our fight for freedom been compromised by one or two fools? Is there anyone willing to stand up and be counted for the sake of common folks? There must be one brave being willing to serve willingly for the unforgotten. Is there one person willing to demonstrate a reason why our life is equal in faith and worth? But wait; there comes one brave spirit willing to redeem the faith lost. He embraces hope with his Sword, fighting for the rights of all. It only takes one delicate flower to spread their gems along the way.

Look around!
Enjoy the blessings from God

Time written by JJB

Time when the world is filled with demanding expectations, I am solely lost. As time moves forward, we as people have defaulted and surrendered our thoughts to mindless games. Carless whispers we try to retrieve but with no direction of recourse. Are there any ideas worth fighting for? Are words said to camouflage our obsession with ourselves? Where have the power of words and motivation gone? Money and greed have power, but they sit on the sideline while fear unleashes the spoils of this wicked, wicked world, deterring the state of the union and replacing hope with fear. **Love is not owed us but simply an opportunity;** it is a pleasure that only a few will obtain and conquer. Peace has no refuge or place if the walls of opportunities have been blocked by silly speculators. Unmask the hidden agenda and recapture time. Release it from its prison! There is no refuge, as time lies in space, all alone, untamed, mocking mankind.

We live in fear not by choice
but by the uncertainities of
what will come

No Regrets Written by Jamey Wilkins

There's too much

Ahead of me

Too many traps

Potholes

Snares, Speed bumps

Strategically placed

To knock me out of the race

I've slipped. Tripped,

Fell on my face but each time

I learned. I grew.

So the next time

I knew

To sidestep

Jump

Slow down

I have to stay alert

To prevent myself

From being hurt

From being attacked

I have no time

To look back

Change written by JJB

Only one person can change the character of

one's fate.

Only one person can fight the battle with a

thought. Only one person can assume the role

of a leader. Facing twisted roads ahead,

Struggling through coils and bumps that lie

ahead. Only I can travel through this single

circle.

I am a man written by JJB

Blood bathed in tears, it seems like decades ago. They have walked in the shadows of the ones that had come before me, screaming for fairness, as they roamed the streets, covered in sheets. They are cowards because they put on a disguise, let them stand as a man for their beliefs without covering up there hate with white sheets. I walk steady and firm because I am who I say I am, **a Man.** What constitutes a Man, why am I still considered a boy? If I walk like a man, let me be what I am, **a Man**. Why do you call me out of my name if I don't have the strength to work longer hours, when I am aching and my body is sore? Why can't I ride my Mercedes along the road without being stopped and interrogated for hours or so? Why am I considered less of a man because I dare to challenge the ill fate of my brothers, who were falsely accused and now live a life behind bars, for what they truly don't know? Can't I rest for a while, without people staring, accompanied with the sound of a sirens, when I walk out my door? Why can't I move into your neighborhood without pressure from my friends fearing I am not who I am. All I ask, all I want, is to be a Man!

Successful Failure written by Jamey Wilkins

I wanna make it

I swear I do

But I know I won't

It seems like

Fate won't allow me to

No matter

How hard I try

I fail

No matter

How sincere I am

How determined I am

I just can't get past

My past

Mr. Freeze
by Jamey Wilkins

A mother

No father

A brother

No sister

A daughter

No son

A heart

No love

See the Light by Earnest Jenkins

Seeing the sun shine on a raining day but we are blinded by choices. We are blind to the world around us; we stand on the brink of darkness that control our days and nights. We hold on to the blind spots that stop us from seeing the world. If we only look inside, we will see the Light.

Black Man by Earnest Jenkins

The man I am as an African American man, will I remain the same as I am? To an unjust world that doesn't' want to change

But in time I will grow and change who I am? Many years will pass by but will I accept the man I am

Will I blame this world for the man that I have become?

As each day passes and new experiences in life happens, will these new experiences change the man inside of me? As the sun rises and the sun se, I will always be the man that God made me to be

   I am what I am, A Man

Fragments written by Gidget E. Seaborne

Sitting here going nowhere

What am I to do?

My mind is so overwhelmed.

Fragments of times, places, sites,

Flowing in and out. What am I to do?

Wondering why I cannot seem to

put a handle on it. Wondering why I am still

here? Is there a purpose? Is there a hope?

Sitting here going nowhere

What am I to do?

Hope rides on the petticoat

of another day

Repercussions written by Jamey L. Wilkins

Motivation

Spurned by education

Inspired by the history

The obstacles overcome

The hurdles leapt

The mountains climbed

The blood shed

The leaders dead

Fearless they stood

So intrepid I will stand

Proud to be a black man

In the Midst of Darkness written by JJB

In the midst of darkness, adorned among a pine tree, a vacant plant evolves, overflowing with fruits and colored leaves, as the light shines from heaven, it seems to be awe-struck by the sun's beauty. The frogs and the grasshoppers flee to the forest as the hunters charge on to hunt and capture the beautiful statuette fawn hiding behind the trees. The moment is still, only silence remains, and then, there is a drop of dew smothering through the rain. The hours are winding down; it is about time to go, but the moment of pleasure is still amongst us, and the excitement is more than a person can score. The forest is entrenched with such marvelous greeneries

from sight to sight.. A landscape impressive

by far, a place enthralled with dreams.

It help me scope amidst the darkness, in a

world filled with beauty and peace.

Family

The thread that ties us by blood

Being in Love written by JJB

This is my testimony of love, from morning, noon, and night. My thoughts are intertwined with raw emotions as I remembered the sparkle of excitement as his hands gently touched my flesh. I was powerless to move for fear this special moment would end. Mesmerized by his voice, I became overwhelmed with a tingling sensation. Consumed with his charisma, my heart increased it rhythms while I was fixated with his every move. Only he had the power to control me. My life had no meaning without the warm fragrance of his body. How can I soften the illusion of my heart without causing this aroma to dissolve? I gave you too much authority, the authority to make me happy. Only a fool will give up their control.

Please give me my life back!

"No!" The Chase yelled back.

"You lost it when you fell so madly and deeply in love." Ha, Ha, ha

The sun shines not because of our works, but because of the compassion of God

Heir written by Jamey Wilkins

My feet hurt

And I've not taken one step

My back aches

And I've not received one lash

My heart is broken

And I've not yet loved

How can this be?

Because pain is hereditary

I remembered by JJB

She smiled when she gave me a bath, only a baby, but nevertheless a child.

Gazing up at her loving eyes, I smiled.
My first walk, I wiggled and wobbled, she guided me with both hands with a smile.
My first words, "DaDa,"
But she took no offense, she picked me up and kissed me lovingly on my cheeks. My first day at school when she had to leave, I cried out a loud scream because fear was in my eyes. She nervously gave me to my teacher. She stared backwards with an uneasy smile. When I felt pain from a hurt, she gave me a hug with loving arms, saying "It's alright my beautiful child." I looked at her; this time it was me who smiled. The day of my

graduation, my heart was beating faster than a mile, but when I looked out in the audience, there proudly taking pictures was my mom, looking at me with a heartfelt smile. Now, I'm grown, and I have a child. I hope I can be half the woman my mother was to me. Looking down at my daughter, I'm so proud to be a mom; it's a pleasure watching my little girl smile.

Ghetto Language written by Jamey Wilkins

I communicate

More effectively with my fists

I can only seem

To get my point across

With sharp objects

I am better understood

More clearly heard when a trigger is pulled.

I've learned violence

It's a motivational speaker, while peace

Is a boring monotone

If I ask politely, I am ignored, if I beg, I am

scorned, if I say nothing, I am oppressed

If I curse…I am paid attention to

Power to do what you say by JJB

How many piles of wood do I have to chop and stockpile, before the marauder realize that *I'm a force of nature* that can't be rechained or demonized. How many more bridges do I have to jump and avoid, before the chaser realize that this goal in my heart was meant to be nurtured the day I was born. To be able to walk this path and retrace another day, I petitioned the counterfeiters to stay out of my way. If people only realize that life don't *owe them a thing*.

Life only waits until maturity to claim the fame and tally the score, then it's a game of chance if you want more. Chin up and seek other direction! Maturity takes time, sometimes it's a waiting game. But if you choose your path wisely, and control your speech, you will gain control whenever you speak.

The Essence of Fear written by Jamey Wilkins

Trying to hurry home, walking up the street at

night. Then all of a sudden, you hear

footsteps coming behind you.

Glance over your shoulder

But there's no trace of anyone, you

Walk faster. It seems as if the footsteps pick

up the pace and begin to run. You start

trotting. But it seems like they're galloping.

You're hollering. Turn around and nobody's

following. Heart racing, you finally make it to

your door step. Whew! It's over

Then, somebody taps you on your shoulder

Helpless written by Jamey Wilkins

I converse with the deaf

But I don't think they're hearing me

Explained my problems to a paraplegic

But I don't think he feeling me

I traveled with the lame

But they don't keep up

I tried to listen to a mute

But he won't speak up

I'm stuck

What did I do to make them treat me this

way?

That is how I feel

when people expect more from me

than I am able to give.

Who Are You by Jamey Wilkins

I thought I knew you

I honestly believed you listened, and

understood me

But you were only looking for contradictions.

You smile

But for some strange reason it resembles a

sneer. Who are you?

I wonder sometimes if your motives are

sincere, my true friend

I considered the bond we share as sacred.

How can such a lovely façade conceal so

much hatred? Who are you? As I look closer,

I think I finally see who you are

You are a reflection of me

Priceless memories written by Jamey Wilkins

Traveling backwards

Helps me move forward

Surviving the present

By living in the past

Remembering the golden days

I wonder what happened

Was it simply fool's gold?

That turned my neck green

Was I just transfixed by the beautiful gleam.

Nah, it was 24 karat

It just got stolen and replaced

With a worthless fake

But I can't discard it because it is all I have to

remind me of how it use to be

What Counts written by Jamey Wilkins

You know I love you right

If you don't, I apologize

For not allowing my actions

To express the feelings I have inside

Maybe I haven't tried

But I thought I did

And isn't it the thought that counts?

I'll be There written by JLW

I may procrastinate

I may hesitate

But I will never break

My stride

Cause I am never fake

Just to set it straight

In case you thought

I lied

You can set a date

I may be late

But you can bet ya fate

On one thing, If you set and wait

Til the stress abate

One of these days

I'm coming!

True Lies written by Jamey Wilkins

What the majority perceives

To be true

Is what the majority believes

Even if it's a lie

Wisdom prevails

Where ignorance fails

But you cannot fail

If you never try.

**Senseless written
by Jamey Wilkins**

Through the eyes of a man

Through the eyes of a girl

Through the eyes of a nut

In the eyes of a squirrel

Through the eyes of a snail

As it slides through the world

From the eyes of a rock

That's disguised as a pearl

With the ears of a bat

I can hear where you at

I can sense when you tense

Like a hound with no scent, Aimless

A gun with no barrel, Stainless

Still, I feel, it's painless

Probably written by JLW

Have you lost the ability

To show your sensitivity?

Have all your emotions

Been worn away by erosion?

Have you become an automation?

Answering questions, how you ought to

respond? Asking things like, "How you

doing?" When you don't give a damn how he

doing. You're probably foul

When things go wrong

Sarcastically, you probably smile

If the answer to any of these questions was

yes. You're probably a mess. You're probably

depressed.

Taste and See written by Geraldine Jenkins

Taste the sweet honey drops on the flowers

Lovely adorned with feathers designed like insects

This scenery is forever printed in my memories

When memories of changes have withered, our love will never fade

Flowers bloom, as seasons change

Let us taste and see this beauty.

Progress Onward
by Geraldine Jenkins

Mountain bound toward the peak of his career, frail but he climb on, He stepped on all the noses and toes of family and friends to progress toward his goal. But he fails to rest, inch by inch, he climbed the ladder to success; his riches undefined. Once there, he met the chill side of the test for his success. The mission for success corrupted his mind that finally killed his body that laid gently in the parlor. There was no one to mourn or cry because he stepped on all the nice people along the way; the ones who truly cared.

**Love found by
Geraldine Jenkins**

Why is my heart longing?

To love, as noon rises above the heart, it

means you are in love. Many seas away in the

Blue Moon in a distant place far from the

dwelling of the lonely heart, love surge

beyond the sweet rage of old father time.

With waves of passion, trembling, conquering

the hope of endless, restless time. I sit lonely,

waiting to find a willing heart that will ease my

pain to stop my bleeding heart. It might come

as a shadow, it might come before day, but I

will sit by my window and wait, hoping I will

see his face.

Respect written by Jamey Wilkins

As we stroll, I focus my eyes on her

Inattentive to skimpy attire, as temptation

walks by. I erase negative connotations,

degrading her being.

Remove explicits from my vocabulary.

Flirtatious actions diminish. Blown away with

the wind. A grin replaces anger. A violent

force never touches her soul. Untold is the

story of respect, extinct in repulsive ways. My

grandmother, my sister, my mother, my aunt

my wife, my daughter

Demand it. Respect those who enabled you to

be. They deserve it!

Through the Eyes of the Warrior
written by Jamey L. Wilkins

Victory is so elusive

Nearly impossible to get a good aim on it. I

give chase, but whether I trot or gallop. I still

never seem to gain on it

I'm weary, I'm weak, I'm tired

It hurts to take each and every breath

Yet I tell myself "only one more to go"

After each and every step

Odds against me it seems hopeless

Wounded from a near kill

By law, my body should've collapsed. Yet it

operates off of sheer will. There are too many

hopes and dreams placed on my fragile

shoulders. But it's a weight I gladly bear. For

it is the plight of a true soldier, If I don't

stand, who will? When it is clear that someone must, that's why I trudge on relentlessly. After victory's scent from dawn til dusk, I cannot fail, I will not fail. I know it can be done. Even if I don't achieve it myself, this battle can be won. So victory, you may as well submit. Though I'm no follower or leader, what makes me a warrior? It's simply that I'm a believer

Being a Man Written by Earnest Jenkins

Look around you and see

At the beginning of time

Do you see yourself as a man?

But yet, you cannot stand alone

You tried so hard to impress others

"Be a man!" Look around you

At the beginning of time, You were born to

win but you decided to fail

You became the Man!

Look around you! The world is not so pretty

now. Someone realized that you were a

winner but you gave up, Who are you?

Web of Lies written by JJB

My body is woven down in a web of deceit.
Why does the truth ridicule me? I try to tell the truth.
But society wants to hear a lie,
I say to you my friend, I'm honest. While descending into a web of deceit, my flesh is beaten down. I hunger for remorse, but my mind is feeble. Questioning myself, I ask, is there any exquisite delight in the truth? How can I trust my integrity when it speaks falsehood, a commonality that I've lost along the way. My speech is twisted, as the web of lies swallows my tongue
I am caught up in a world of trickery but wait; I will be honest and speak. There is no truth

unless there are others around to hear me

speak, so I will remain quiet.

How can I overcome the hardships this world

offers because the truth is unheard of?

My web of lies have destroyed my integrity as

I attempt to compose myself, as the

sun set in the blazing heat of the day, I will try

my best to murmur the truth before it gets

caught up in my web of lies.

Wisdom written by Gidget E. Seaborne

She struts like a queen."

She is phenomenal.

She is my teacher.

One who exceeds excellence

One who has strengths beyond my comprehension.

One who reaches for and obtains the untouchable.

One who is wise beyond her years.

One who I learn from

I marvel at her insight.

She is phenomenal.

She is my teacher.

To Know written by Jamey Wilkins

That is all I ever wanted. No amount of money or material possession can compare to this intangible ability. As I look back on my life, I realize that if I had only known my life would have turned out different. If I had known that, even though it looked cool, associating with thugs, gangsters and drug dealers, I would be considered one, even though I was neither…

If I had known that being in their presence I would unconsciously pick up some of their bad characteristics such as, being disrespectful to my elders, smoking and drinking which would further tarnish my image and creditability…..

If I had known that school was a blessing instead of a burden. That social studies (boring!) actually applied to me,
that English would help me communicate more effectively, maybe, just maybe, I would not be where I am today, incarcerated.
It's funny, because during my search to find guns and knives to protect myself from those who I willingly hung around, the most powerful weapon on earth was so easily accessible. More powerful than a machine gun, it even surpasses the strength of a nuclear weapon. The most valuable thing costs absolutely nothing, knowledge. It is something that everyone can possess, but no one can truly own.

Yeah, If I had only known…

But hold up, the beauty of knowledge is that it is never too late to acquire it. Your past is just that, your past. It's over with, it can't be changed but it can be converted from a foolish mistake to a humbling lesion. Learn from it, so your future will not be a re-enactment of it. Education is essential to growth, so if you want to become a grown man, a grown woman, and be considered by others as one, first you must be willing to learn. The foundation of learning is listening: to your parents, your teachers, your conscience, to people who have been down the road you are just now approaching.

If only I had listened I would not have to actually feel fire to know it burned. I would not have to retrace my footsteps to get back where I already was before I made this wrong turn. If only I had known…..

Knowledge is infinite and unlike money or material things once you use it you still have it. You can learn from everything and everyone in existence, even me.

Everything you ever wanted is within your grasp, all you have to do is reach out and grab it, be it that next book or magazine. Now I know you're thinking who is he, to tell me anything, how does he know." Well, I know because I was once your age, I know because I learned through trial and error, I know because I started to listen. As for who I am…..

Ha! I go by the name Experience

No Cure written by Jamey Wilkins

Terminally sick

Eternally ill

Yearning a fix

Of infirmary pills

If I had one wish

I 'd wish to be healed

Cause pain is the only

Condition I feel

What did I do

Why am I cursed

When will it end

Why does it hurt

Hoping to live

Anxious to die

Too late to care

Too weak to cry

No turning back

No way to run

It seems I forgot

The meaning of fun

It won't go away

Though I pray and I plead

Inflicted afflicted

With a fatal disease

The Road to Riches written by Jamey Wilkins

Being stripped of it

Made me realize their value

I used to not care

They came a dime a dozen

Now out of a dozen

I can't even get a dime

Never had I risked my heart

I always played it safe

That's the way playas play

But I don't wanna be a playa no more

Cause won't nobody play with me

I'm a grown man now

I have no time for childish games

I want to experience the real thing

Now that I've been broke

I know the beauty the strength

The power a woman possesses

I desperately want to cherish

To adore, to pour out my empty heart

And love her

For only that priceless possession

Can make me rich

This time once she's mine

I'll never let her go

Wasted years written by JJB

Tick, Tock, years turned into decades
Old father time, where have you departed?
Reality seems so far away.
Once, I was a voyager; a person without any direction.
I'm older now with no more seeds to sow.
Times are harsh; words of literacy are foreign to me. As the sweat falls off my face, I seek redemption. For years, my weakness enslaved me and seduced me into a coma like state.
There is hope I say, hope that my life has some decree.
Bitterness swells inside of me as my soul cries out for relief. Tears only for the silent years, the time when I was trying to find my way.

I spent years climbing the corporate ladder
While I neglected to enjoy the light of
happiness. At last, I see the rainbow hidden
behind the clouds.
Even though the light is camouflaged amidst
the clouds, I see blue, red, orange and white.
Years wasted, or hidden from my sight.

Upbringing written by Jamey Wilkins

Profiled as so wild, uncouth

Young youth

Unaware of where

They came from

Unaware of what

They're made of

Some say they gave up

Blame it on the father

The one who didn't bother

Or maybe the mother

The one who stayed uncovered

Half naked half crazy

Why did she have babies?

Why was she allowed?

Why not?

Who told her she shouldn't

Not you, not me

But the media cause what is portrays

Has turned boys gay

Women into dykes

And they actually believe it's alright

Alright, okay, I give

I'ma let you live

Passivity has birthed

The worse of the worse

What happened to the rod

Who said spare it?

The same people that can afford to

I can't afford not to

So I won't

And please don't

Bring ya wild, uncouth

Young youth

Unaware of where

They came from

Around my sons

Around my daughters

because I am a father

Who doesn't care if I bother?

My child or not

They gon' grow up right

Conscious about life

Respectful

And I bet you

They pass it on

One Way by Jamey L. Wilkins

Once said

Words cannot be taken back

They only travel one way

So when speaking One must be careful

What one say, the tongue is the road

The voice is the car. The mind is the engine.

The oil is the thought that lube up the brain.

When designing a sentence

Emotion press the gas. While the conscience

controls the brakes

When feelings are at stake, be careful what

you say

Because once said words cannot be taken

back. They only travel one way

Sins of This World written by JJB

Hypocrisy is the sin of this world

Haughtiness cause people to rise and fall

cleaver as a fox, they lay waiting for any sign

of weakness

Pretending to be amicable to appease the

situation of the lost

Hatred is brazen on their tongues. Callous

thoughts arcane (secretly) hidden

On their pillow at night. Avarice, has

destroyed their soul

Why do men and women want more than

they are worth when they speak?

Candor words are often spoken, only to

appease the followers of the unforgotten.

Why do we have to debase the young and the guiltless? While the character of the people we love, we debate. Sarcastically, I giggled. In my demure state, my eyes watered.

I am the finest of the fine.

My followers will destroy the weak with their blades.

Where are the fools, the ones that wouldn't open the door when I needed food, shelter, and wisdom? People scorned me until there was only a shell of a person left.

Looking in the mirror, I see only a shadow, and in its place there stood all the sins of this world basking in all their glory

Ready and eager to take my place

You and they written by Earnest Jenkins

I wanted to do things my way. You tried to stop me. They support you in your attempt. I was in charge. You stood in my way. They support you in your stand. You and They came together. I recognized that I could not win. So, I became the you, and they became the I, YOU and THEY

Me Against Me written by Jamey Wilkins

My hand my chest my leg

Things that can be crushed

My love, my knowledge, my fears

Things that can't be touches

My heart my lung my brain

Things that are my physical

My mind

 my spirit my soul

Things that are invisible

Two components of self

One pulling one pushing

Material and immaterial

One true and one crooked

Constant struggle between me

My heart and my pride

Give or take

bend or break

It's hard to decide

Ironic, trying to live

And let neither get the best of me

Catch 22 cause either one I pick

Will eventually be the death of me.

Sometimes remaining silent
Is the best remedy"

Lone Wolf written by Jamey Wilkins

Hatred, jealousy, envy

Manifests themselves in me

So I erupt spewing volcanic acid at bastards

Lies, threats to kill them afterwards

Can't put my hands on them

So I assassinate their character

But when all is "said and done."

When all of them are gone

I find I still have those traits

In me when I'm all alone

Real written by Jamey Wilkins

To me

Real doesn't exist

When everyone

Can look at the same thing

And see different

Real is an illusion

It's not a lie

But it's not the truth

For it can't be proven

I can't tell you. What you see

Neither can you tell me what I

All we can do

Is look in the same direction

And hope the reality doesn't pass us by

Me and You, You and me written by Jamey Wilkins

If you could see thru my eyes

I wonder how you would deal with

The pain I hold inside

I wonder if you would look at you

The way I look at you

And see the same things I do

Things I wouldn't do

Then I wonder why

…Hmmm let me try

To look thru your eyes

And see if I would cry

Probably so

But only if I were you

Because then I could do things

That I wouldn't see

Yet we both see the same

How? Well let me explain

To you I'm a disappointment

If you think that that's a lie

You'd be deceiving yourself

Cause I can see it in your eyes

That I didn't achieve

What you know I could achieve

If only I had believed

What you know I should believe

Have considered that

I'm only being myself

And that you see more in me

Than I see in myself

To me you are a disappointment

If you wish that's a lie

You'd be deceiving yourself

Can't you see it in my eyes?

That I expect so much from you

Things I know you can achieve

But you don't want to know

You only want to believe

Maybe I should consider

That you're just being yourself

Do I see more in you

Than you see in yourself

Now do you see how we see

The same but differently

I see what is but you see

What you wish it would be

Have you ever just sat back

And listened to me

And understood what I said

Paid attention to me

I know, I know, true

I never listened to you

So who am I to question

Some of the shit that you do

Remember you said

I have book sense but no

common sense

Where I see rare pennies

You only see common sense

I feel you are ashamed of me

And deep down that anger me

Why not accept me for me

And not be intent on changing me

I'll never be ashamed of you

And don't think I'm blaming you

Actually I'm blaming me

For not being what I claim to be

But you are me, I am you

We are one, we are two

When I let you see thru me

I would like to see thru you

Even though I'm gone away

My heart still pumps your blood

If you took the blood away

My heart'll still want ya love

Lovers of the Flesh by JJB

Lovers of the utmost qualities

Passion drove me to overlook whatever

boundaries there were, yes!

Desires of the flesh conquered all my doubts

Was I a lover in the moment, awe! With

raging desires, let me think.

Finally, I was caressed, after years of absentee

and empty beds, now my flesh is warm from

the body of my lover, will this passion last

forever? Who knows?

But for today, my cup is filled from the thirst

of his kisses.

A mother's plead to child to be strong written by JJB

Momma, momma, I can't!

Child speak out! Tell them they are wrong!

But momma, I can't!

Be strong my child!

But momma, what will happen if I protest?

Honey, the hour is near; our burdens must be cast out.

We must rise out from the ashes to voice our troubles, there are no more slaves.

What do you mean momma?

To let things stay the same denotes not being a part of the change.

Oh, oh

So, if I'm calm, if my thoughts go unheard, there will be no change.

No, my child.

Then I must rise up from the fear that

common man/woman bounds me

Momma, do you think I can ever conquer my

fear, to challenge the wrongs?

Yes! My child

Because you represent the future of all

Human Beings

It is the hope that closes or opens each door

You are the future that bounds all men

accountable to their own deeds

To live in Peace written by JJB

Peace, this is a word few get the priviledge to enjoy. Life is broken by hunger and pain. Neighbors, or foes, it seems that life is a game. Are we destined by our animal instinct, to be a wild beast or a prey! Do we want to die from the knife that probes our backs from the shadows of our so-called friends, or to live in peace? It's 'an opportunity that we all must search for, it's a decree that we all must abide by. It's a dream that we all must cherish and uphold. It's the factual knowledge that distinguish us from the wild animals of the prey or the people who walks the street on their excursion to find peace. All I want is To live, To pray and To die in Peace

Love doesn't happen by Chance by JJB

We smiled

We danced

We enlightened each

other about our thoughts

I'm in love

L-O-V-E

No time to waste

Gotta get married!

Um

Such a fool,

Instant romance

Means, instant Pain

Love doesn't happen by chance

Love is a reality that feeds the heart.

What does the word Friend means?
By JJB

Rugged roads I faced, struggling to find my place

But I made it, did you my so-called friend help me? Ah, ah

Please! I begged. Can you buy this, can you at least help me with my flyers and my promotions, after all, it's your area of expertise. Call me back later, you stated!

Tried to bring about awareness about my passion, negativity was all I got. What're you doing that for! Bluntly, you stated.

Aren't we inspired to be good citizens, to go after the American Dream?

We as Blacks have long forgotten the plights that our forefathers have Fought so hard for.

The right to unite, and the right to come together to solicit a bond that excite and unify. But we have become so attuned to the way things are.

We are lazy when it comes to fighting for causes that affect us all.

We expect others to fight our battle while we sit and watch, sipping

beers or sodas at night.

Then, we cry for justice when it hits home.

Well, you did nothing!

Now, you are another black person gone.

Why should I help you now, my hands are tied.

Your mouth was foreign from my ears when I needed you. When I needed a confidant, where were you?

But I made it, so I'm returning the errand, if you had asked, if you had simply cared about me, and not my accomplishments, things might be different.

The burden of proof, Awe, there wouldn't have been an argument in your case.

But some say, "a tooth for a tooth," is the answer, My dear friend.

But I'm not made from the same cloth, if we can't forgive, we will never grow.

Ah, I will see what I can do.

Let me be for real. Today is a new day, if we pull together and not **act beyond our means, because we are the same, not by the segregated** factors that surrounds our life, but by common factors that connect us my dear friend.

Africa We Hear Your Cry written by JJB

Trouble placed on the burden of a nation but many countries have passed you by. Many sit in silence, with thoughts of unbelief, emotionless to the call. These people are hurting! They are starving and dying every day. Just step up for humanity, they are human beings not animals.

We see pictures of kids starving, their stomachs are enclaved with empty hopes. Violence in every aspect of their life. There are massacres disguised in all forms; it's bleeding their minds of the property of life. A child's innocence is lost every day among the oppressor's breast. Many of them are scared for the rest of their lives. We can't reject their petitions because it is for humanity at best. It takes more than a wonder or just a simple how do you do. No one person can do it all. It takes thousands or even millions to answer the call. The recurring calls to educate people. It is our duty to help fight this plight. We can't remove our conscious and say it is not our cause.

I live my story by Josephine j. Bridgers

I live my story

I walk the steps that others before me have bedded down, so that I will be able to have opportunities. That's what has silenced my tears and "lifted me up" beyond my means.

Even though I sit amidst the chaos, I rise beneath the dust that falls beneath my feet. I Rise to become not just a woman of needs to a person of self-worth. I think about the vision of dreams lifted up on the bellies of slave's while giving nutrition to the master's child. They were lifted by the spirit of hope.

I Rise from being a mortal woman to a woman that doesn't behold to doubt or Fear. I live my story not for the world to embrace but for all those runaway slaves who refused to be whipped or chained anymore.

I live my life in remembrances of the Underground Railroad because without their Hearts opened, doors would remain closed.
I live my story for the ones hidden in the wilderness but wake up in the dawn of the night, Praising God for his grace.
Yes, I know you are hurting but "you are not alone"

Rise up from the fear that bounds men's
tongues saying, you can't
and replace it with, I can!
That is why I live my story
To inspire others because without
A path opened up for me,
There would be no stories
There would be no dreams

Insight for author's piece, Paying your dues

Insight in writing this piece was, so many times we value materialistic things instead of honoring God, we sometimes forget that his mercy allows us to be and strive.

When the author write, she try to base her thoughts on these themes: "A time to live, rejoice, cry, and a time to die." These are her premises in which she cultivated her inspirations.

Even though, our choices are no joking matter, the author adds humor with a twist.

Paying my dues written by JJB

Paying my dues were easy on earth, now I must wait at the pearly gates to see if it were enough? The pastor preached a good sermon but was it enough to make up for my life on earth? Boy, wasn't that sermon good? it almost made me want to get up and walk out. But I didn't see any tears shed. The building was sparcely packed or was there a lot of people? I can't remember. Where were all my family members? Were they in the other room? I can't remember! Where was the lady down the street with that beautiful purple hat? Oh, did I forget to tell her, "Hi" when her husband lost his job? I hurried past her because I didn't want to hear her beg. Can't remember, Can't remember. With money, there is fame, maybe I will buy my way to heaven. Let me see, I'm riding my Mercedes in the pearly gates now, Aint my ride fine? It was easy living on Earth without a care, because money made things happen. There was no time to comfort my neighbors, no time to say hey. The Bible, you got to be kidding! I didn't have time for that! It was work as usual, reading the Bible would have been time consuming. Please pass me a glass of wine so I can chill! My day at work was tiresome as always. Busy as a bee, no time to treat anyone with kind words. But I had time for my money and the luxury it offered. It was worth more than a Hi or The Bible. But this road is so wide, people have so much room. But why are they not speaking? Why do they look so sad? The road ahead seems even gloomier. There is a hollow look on all the people's faces, where are we going I asked? Everyone stopped and looked back at me. "Look around you, they said." "Do the people look happy?" "No! I replied." "Well you know now, all your life' you built your fortune, never giving God any time, the path you've chosen was the wrong one. Now you are on the road with the lost souls, there will be a judgment. You tried to buy yourself into Heaven, being silly, riding your Mercedes trying to get into the pearly gates.

Most of us weren't that dumb! We rode our bikes attempting to look humble. Then you tried to write a check and guess what? Your money was returned, no address for worldly goods. But, but, I have money. Everyone looked back, "we're too sad to laugh but you just baked the cake."

All your time you spent honoring your worldly possessions, do you honestly think God gonna find favor in you?

Get back in the back of the line!

Stop smiling you clown! Where do you think you going?

An Angel in Waiting by JJB

Who was my brother?

Was he a man without flaws?

No, because he wasn't perfect, but he was the kindness and sweetest person I've ever known.

Whatever flaws he had I didn't observed because of my own flaws. Which I am still counting. It seemed to me that my brother was an angel in waiting the minute he was born. He had a presence that welcomed you regardless of your background. Have you ever seen a person that had a presence that was so extraordinary, something that can't be described?

If I painted you a picture of how he was, would you believe me?

To his family, he was an angel in waiting, because his spirit continues to live on in all our hearts and minds.

I remember his wit, I remember his gentleness and most of all, his laughter. He had what people today called the It factor, but whatever he had, he had it with that amazing smile. He was very artistic; his artworks were breathtakingly beautiful; you could see his designs throughout his home. He also had a couple of his paintings highlighted on the wall at his job.

Who was this person, we called uncle, brother, father, son and friend?

How can you describe a person whose sole purpose in life was living not for himself but living his life according to God's Words.

He lived his life in complete harmony with God's vision. But he is gone now, only for a short while. He was born from the flesh of a woman. A father he respected in the midst of his wrongs. But, nevertheless, he loved him because he was a loving son. When I get lonely, I think about my brother, a breeze gusting by that wrap me up in his arms saying "my dear sister please be strong!" But in that same breath, I see butterflies saluting, me, saying, "your brother is finally home."

He was an angel in waiting. In the midst of his darkness when he was experiencing discomfort, he ministered to others despite experiencing pain. He lived his life rich in love; he was an angel in waiting. A gift given to our family as a token of God's love. His life's journey speaks his works because today, in the shadow of our hearts, I see butterflies and it reminds me of my brother's amazing spirit. The day he passed, all things ceased in their tracks. My heart broke into several pieces but then it mended together as I thought about my brother, he was a gift to my mother because his spirit echoed love. But I thank God for his mercy and his grace, hopefully one day, I will see my brother again.
He was an angel in waiting

No regrets by JJB

Yesterday, I gave him all his flowers Today, I'm at peace. Wordless I sat and pondered. There are so many things, I wished I had addressed. Even though we had our differences, He was my oldest brother and I loved him with every single breathe. Although, I said it so many times, utterance from my mouth was not enough. It's the everyday things we sometimes take for granted like seeing the person's face or calling to say hey. No words can replace what I truly feel. But God is a loving God, if we cultivate his teachings by watering our knowledge, our faith will definitely grow.

The Game changing
by Earnest Jenkins

It is time to move on

If we see the sun today

We are blessed if we see the moon tonight.

We live for another night. Time can be on our

side but the game changing moment lives in

our life forever. What day is it?

I really don't know.

I Searched for endless moments. Sometimes

the price depends on whether I live or die.

In a world of confusion, we are always

searching for that moment.

The moment or time, we can be what we

want to be. But the questions lie in our heart

That determines what our responses will be

Envisioning Rosa Parks

I wrote this piece envisioning the night before Rosa Parks got on the bus. These are my thoughts about the suspense leading up to this heroic feat. I tried to visualize what she was experiencing and to bring light to what was going through Rosa's mind the night before the famous stand for freedom. Even though, I was not in Rosa's predicament, I used my imagination to convey the significance of what was about to happen. Can you imagine being in this woman's shoes for a second? After years of planting the seeds of despair, saying that Blacks were heathens, and less than animals, this form of brainwashing takes years to undo. This struggle will not end overnight, but we must start a new day supporting each other by forging new ideas. We must use whatever platform we have to inform because we as a people have yet to overcome.

Envisioning Rosa Parks before she got on the Bus by JJB

The night before she rode the bus I envisioned the fear Rosa Parks had because she was only human, but she knew emancipation was worth fighting for. Would she reach her destination or not? This time it was crucial that she follow through with her plan and not give up; she probably thought about all the runaway slaves beaten and killed just for rising up against their master's hands. When she took her daily walks, she saw hatred everywhere, signs saying, Colored not allowed. This inhumane treatment of black folks, she couldn't understand why it was ever allowed.

I imagine she thought about all the slaves and what they went through while providing nutrition to their masters's children. Rosa was probably overwhelmed with thoughts, but she believed in the power of God. Rosa probably questioned, why did the color of her skin excite misperceptions? She probably thought about all the things she had endured, and why it was so relevant that she now make her move. I envisioned Rosa weighing her options on whether it was worth the risk of losing everything she had worked so hard to get. I envision her finally coming to the decision that she couldn't lose something she never had. Nevertheless, the night before, Rosa probably couldn't get any sleep. What if she got weak and became afraid, then the cycle of injustice would continue to tip the scale? She probably thought about her husband, would he be saddened by her actions? I imagine she was scared, what if she got beaten or lynched. These are some of the questions I envision she asked herself in the wee hours of the night. The next morning, she probably kneeled down and said a heartfelt prayer. She knew that the power of God was greater than what men could do to her flesh. She probably could feel God's holy spirit preparing her for this task, but most of all, she had confidence that this mission was about to be won because she believed in the power of prayer. When everything fails, God is always there. I envisioned she put on her glasses, took her Bible from her purse and took a deep breath and proceeded to prepare for whatever came next.. After weighing her options, she waited and waited until she saw the bus. Armed with her Bible, this brave soul stepped on the bus. **No longer a willing participant because she was someone daughter and someone mate that made her an heir. After her, there would be others taking up the reigns paving their way to freedom!**

Friends by author

She was my friend; her hair was straight and my hair was curly. We laughed and played when we were together; she was who she was and that was alright. We never viewed ourselves as being different, even though, I was black and she was white. When we went to school, neither one of us could understand, but we were besties, not letting our challenges affect us being friends. Sometimes she would cry and say, "I'm sorry my friend, why do they hate you so? You are just like me but only you have darker skin. Then, I would say "that's alright, with your shoulder to lean on, we will fight this cause together." But my white friend's mother got sick and she moved away, I forgot to tell her that I loved her dearly, because she instilled in me hope. That's one of the reasons, I write. When crying was the only way, she would say, "if you let them win, what would you have to fight for," hate isn't a part of God's plan." She lifted me up when people called me names; she would say " how can they love God when they're so filled with rage for a little black girl with pig-tails. She would ball up her fist and hit the wall, saying, "I sorry my little beautiful black friend." My friend's parents taught her love not based on the color of a person's skin. I remembered one time, she stood in the way to avoid me getting hit; this caused a disturbance while some people walked away, I heard someone say "stay out of it, you have privileges because of your white skin." Who would dare hit a little blond hair white girl with cherry ribbons? My friend was beautiful, even though she said she has never seen anyone as beautiful as me. But nevertheless, she was my bestie who didn't judge me based on the color of my skin. Oh my, she was so sweet. What was I to do since my friend was gone? But I remembered what my friend said " Don't you worry your little head a bit. 'You are the best friend I ever had, my beautiful black friend."

Why do they have to label you?

We are the same; we are tied by blood. The same mother, father and same God.

In my books, I try to enlighten people by showing that we are not alone. God put people in our path to help us ride out the storms. For instance, sometimes we don't know how something happen because it seemed so unreal then someone steps in our paths and help guide us toward a better space.

Think Positive by Lillian Jenkins

When there is thunderstorm that darken the beautiful sky, you know the radiant sun will shine again. When there is a winter blizzard that chill you down to your bones, you know our mother earth will cover you with a warm blanket once again. When there is sadness that grips you by the hand and does not seem to want to let go, you know that happiness will glide you away with a sudden mercifulness in perfect timing. So let us think positive no matter what befall us. Because one day all our positive thoughts may bring Joy, may bring happiness, may bring peace and may all your hopes come true.

Feeling by Erica Davis

The doors are locked and the key is within your soul. Your happiness is the light, your anger is bold. Your tears hurt, with pain from the heart. Our mind is dark with fears deep inside the heart. You clutch your chest with the feeling of love. The loss of passionate, affection from the sould. You dreamed of waking-up one day, living in a fairy tale but you and I both know tht this world is more like a living naightmare. The loving world, that you once saw, is almost unrecognizable. Your eyes tend to swell up with thoughts of despair. Your words seem to make no sense when it comes to talking in thin air. The lightning that surrounds the stormy sky is filled with rage. The emotional outrage takes the stage. Happiness is there in the light. Darkness scares it away with fresh delight. But do not be afraid by these harmful emotions for they should not scare you. Who are you to say I cannot! Who are you to say happiness is no longer my friend. You can see straight through the light. A person's mind can be their own private enemy. Do not be afraid to let yourself speak for light is in the air. You shall speak! You unlock the door which was once locked. You unclench your chest which was once held like a pounch. You stop sobbing and crying for now you can speak. Happinesss is within your soul for you to keep!

Guard your heart by Lillian Jenkins

"How do you mend a broken heart is a question many have asked?"

And up to this point it has been a dawning task. Because feelings are involved. Which makes this question hard to solve. However the answer to this question comes from within. Time is the healer but negative thinking is the killer. You see, your heart is not really broken, your mind uses this excuse as a token. In the mind, you control all vital organs. The heart is the most precious, so it should be guarded. So cherish it my friend, and it may ache but with a strong mind, you will be determine not to let it break.

Always Guard your heart

The Reflection of my family by Earnest Lee Jenkins

It is time to move ahead; we have lived a life of many tales from cornfields to cotton fields. Some of of us are still living in the past. We are the Jenkins/Harrison's family; a family that continues to strive through the good and the bad of this generation. We never asked for a lot of things in life; we only asked for what we are owed, freedom to live. We hope for the best and plan for the worse. We are the Jenkins/Harrison's family. We are a proud family. Our struggles have not been fruitless; our pain has only made us stronger. Even though we live in a world brimful with darkness, these are the days we have chosen to make a difference. In a world that seems to flourish with self-hatred, we have exceeded beyond the goals of our forefather. From end to end with an evolution of hope, we continue prosper. We have looked beyond the common ground and jumped over fences that seemed to bind us down. We as a family has continued to strive.

Look around in the midst of us, the gift of life shines among our faces.

Dear Mom by Jamey Wilkins

I am potential in its purest form
I am strength; I am power. I am beauty. I am the future. But I am also a reminder of the past and that's why I won't last. even though I am part of you, I am also a part of them. A part that you are better off without. At least that is what you tell yourself. I am a burden; I am a stumbling block but I am also love, pride and innocence. I am everything you wanted to be. I am helpful yet helpless. I am a childish mistake. The consequence of your risk. I am your harvest. I am Karma. I am an extension of your existence. At least I would've been if you hadn't aborted me. Love always.

A Letter to My Dear Mother

Cultivated by Love

Savored with honey and spice

Topped with morsel with a delicacy of honey plums and rice, she is my loving mother. Her smile lights up the room while her eyes glitter as they shine. She is the best mother ever because she is meek as well as kind. My mother strengths have uplifted our family through the peaks of disaster, rising high as an eagle to fly as the wind breezes by. With her guidance, our family have prospered. She has guided us through endless struggles remaining true to her faith by giving God the honor as the Keeper of the Gate. All the life's lessons we have learned, she has been instrumental in giving us the tool for success. She is the foundation that governs our life; she is our comfort. She created a space where all her children can come and rest. She is more than a mother; she is more than a friend, she is that steady rock that never bends. Her love is endless; she provides unlimited hours because she secretly knows, God is the keeper of the Gate.

Resistance by Jamey L. Wilkins

Pressure is nothing

Pain is nothing

Fear is nothing

Force is nothing

Hate is nothing

Because, freedom is everything

I Walk Alone by Jamey L. Wilkins

No one sees the tears fill to the brim

And leak from the corner of my eye

No one stares, is it because one one cares?

Or is this weakness normal for a guy?

With my head held low, I have nowhere to go.

I watch my feet pummel the ground. I glance

in no direction; I look for no affection. As my

tears start tumbling down only I can taste the

salty embrace of my liquid sorrow. My tongue

goes numb as if it were stung. I don't savor

the favor; I swallow. My stomach fills with

emptiness. Memories range from bitter to

sweet. The thirst of my of my soul remains

unquenched so my spirit continues to weep.

Who can smell the scent of despair?

Intermingled with the aroma of guilt. I

noticed a mare that nostrils did flare and in his eyes I saw only comtempt. The stench of failure pollutes me, engulfs me. I am alone, trouble seems to follow me. As if attracted by my cologne. If anyone says they feel my pain, then I would tell you, at once, they lied. For if it were true when I'm hurt and I'm bruised, tell me, why don't they cry? Lonelinesss touches me, caresses me in the wee hours of the night. I feel remorse for choosing this course but I can't change the past try as I might. Nobody, hears the plip-plop of my tears. Though my ears detect every drop. The bass drum of my heart is missing its spark. And sounds like it's ready to stop. I scream out in frustration. I sob; I sniffle. I whimper; my whole body stiffens. Ashamed at my lack of control, I face the globe. But it seems as if nobody listened. They pay no attention to my condition. And I feel that this needs some explaining. I look to the sky to ask the Lord why. And that's when I realize it's raining.

Let's Get Acquainted written by Jamey L. Wilkins

Cool people embrace me but schooled people hate me. I use people, so only a few people can escape me. You can't shape me, can't mold me, or control me. I have one mission and that is solely to destroy all that is holy.

I've been applied to many guys. I am genocide in disguise. Men/Women devised a scheme now their dreams are being materialized.

Who am I? Ha! Ha! Ha! I am the one you least expected. The one you yearn to have sex with, with whom you'd never use protection. Hold up.... I have a confession.... I just lied! It is not who or where I am for I cannot be characterized.

I am brawny, I am scrawny, I am white, I am black. I am comely, I am homely, I am this, I am that. I am here, I am there, I am lovable, and hatable. I'm in a polygamous relationship so I am always available, from homosexuals to bisexuals to heterosexuals.

The only ones who are questionable are the "I don't have sexual."

Pardon the intrusion, sorry if I've caused confusion, but let me start with the problem and conclude with the solution. It is hard to avoid me seeing that the media is collusion. Unbeknownst to them, of course, are the strategic methods that I'm using. I mingle amongst the "in crowd". I blend in with the stars. The people kids idolize transport me like cars. They take me to your T.V. screens and magazines, cause "sex sells." As evidenced in commercials and the classified section of your XXL"s. They promote me, if you ain't having sex, you aint cool. So once virginity is lost, kids brag about it in school. A bunch of fools, I lure them and majority bites the bait, which exponentially increases the chance of putting their life at stake. My goal is to conquer the globe, but I have to move fast to accomplish it. Condoms slow me down but abstinence is more abstinent. I'm so intelligent I use a different tactic for the celibate. I run rampant in poverty-striven environments where crime and drugs are prevalent. Family problems leave them depressed, it gets stressful through the years. While they are some sort of solace I offer pressure from their peers. It seems the only way to escape the madness is through liquor and wee. That's just the beginning so it really doesn't make a difference to me. Eventually they'll drop their drawers... with luck they'll drop their drawers, if not, that's okay I'll let fate take its proper course. Addiction. The same dosage no longer gives them a buzz. So to achieve their high they change the way that they administer drugs. First they smoked it, then they sniffed it, anything to get lifted. Now I recruit their friends to introduce them to something different. It's just a needle prick, it won't hurt, it may bleed a bit. But it's the quickest way to get high, when you need a fix." And to fit in they just allowed me to enter them, gave me permission to use their body as my instrument. Simpletons.... after I am injected, I remain undetected. By the time I show my face they won't know when or where they were infected. I possess them. Rejection...feelings of depression inspires some to intentionally transmit me to the next man/woman.

Beautifully we enter the club with a fake I.D. Now that we're partners, let's get acquainted, "Hi I'm H.IV."

How to protect yourself? That's a secret I wouldn't normally give away. But I learned that the majority is ignoring me anyway. Some feel that I exist but won't happen to them.

They are so naive and that's why I'm attracted to them.

If you have to have sex I'd suggest you use a condom. I rarely breach the barrier, latex always give me a problem. To be 100% sure obtain from intercourse totally. Then it's virtually impossible for you to be sexually exposed to me. Or you could find a partner, take the test, and practice monogamy. If your partner decides to cheat... well I offer you my apology.

The abuse of drugs will alter your mind state. Often it puts you in a coffin or increases the crime rate. No drugs, no blood, no me. We would never get acquainted and you would never get to know me. But you will see me because I am a slow death imperialized.

Without you, though, some men/women dream cannot be materialized. You are schooled so now you hate me, while cool people still embrace me. I've used people but you are one of the few people who escaped me… for now

The Potential for Greatness by J. Bridgers

When I was a child, I wondered

What was so deep in my soul that made me daydream?

As I reminisced, I think of words my momma use to say,

"Child never mind what people say

You have the potential for greatness.

You are my little prodigy and they can't write you off

So many women have been beaten and cursed

Until their broken bodies surrendered to the callings of the wild

But endure, my child, the taunts, and the roadblocks placed in your path

Raise your head!

Keep on spitting forward greatness with every

Prolific verse of speech written and spoken by men. You are the product of greatness.

Birthed from pain and received with opened hands.

You're my beautiful child.

You are that little girl that rose from the gates of uncertainities to reclaim what others mocked and tried to destroy.

Keep your head high!

Sometimes greatness come with a price

Look up my child!

Don't you hear the calls from the wilderness?

Claim your path now before the lions tear you apart!

Who are you my child?"

The little girl started running. She runs and runs. She lifted her head up high and screams.

"I am, I am, then she spits out, ' I have

the potential for Greatness!"

Your breath is my breath by JJB

You're my breath of life.

Your intoxicating smile is the theme to all my rhythms and poems.

You legitimized my love by allowing me to mirror positivity.

Your awe-inspiring persona allows me to jump over any obstacles giving me super human strength to persevere and regain more strength to battle the climate of time.

Sightless, blinded by your intoxication, I jogged on an escapade trail to an unreal lane.

This mysterious path leads me to the valley of sweet tender notes where silhouette shadows, captivates my curiosity and allures me on.

I see shadowy figures surrounded by waves and notes floating in the air while an enthusiastic soul played Summer Rain.

Such poetic meaning of expression you have given me, intriguing me, you speak with such graceful lyrics. These moments are captured on the tip-toes of the moon's smile in the bliss of the night. Intensifying the scenery of bliss, the squirrels assembled to steal pears from an overflowing tree.

While the dog slept, the tree became vulnerable. The sly squirrels stacked the deck. We laughed as we stared into each other's eyes while taking in the scent of the moon's fragrance.

This delighted all our senses in the breeze of the midnight heat.

A night my breath regained its strength while every minute I savored the smell of my lover's minted breath. Redeeming my yearning to be close in the presence, I embraced this moment.

A time when only a second, time allured the chase of morning. Then night waited for dawn with ecstasy and delight.

Surely, I thought, the ideology of living is so invigorating.

Then all thoughts ceased.

As the Sun rose to a new day

Why Should I Care written by Jamey L. Wilkins

If for me there is no profit

Or nothing I could lose

Why should I care?

When someone else is abused

I eat well; sate my thirst

My pockets are filled with money

So why should I care

If a child is going hungry

I am physically fit

I have no allergies or bad habits

Why should I care?

That so and so is a crack addict

I'm smart, well employed

Life to me has been sweet

Why should I care?

If that old lady can't cross the street

No worries for me or mine

No reason to go out on a limb

So why do I care? Because I could've been one ot them

That Child by JJB

That child

Caused a nation to uncover its hate

That child was a poster child for hate.

That child was profiled and killed

And left him lying in the dirt

That child

Caused people to look at the disparities

In the court system

Making stricter Laws for blacks

While some whites get a pat on their backs

That child

Allowed us to mourn and look for answers

From God

That child

Allowed us to uncover the hidden

Agenda that racism strive as a sore

Running wild

That child

Caused a nation to be divided through racial lines

That child

Cause me to shed tears for my sons

While others sought protection from God

But all and all

That child made a nation realized that we are

Not yet free, free, just to be!

Blood to blood, injustice Takes our own

by JJB

Blood to blood, we are kin

Labor of pain that coats our sins

A dollar bill is less than a penny

A loaf of bread, few is fed.

Blood to blood, no signs of

Change, The fluorescent light

That hides the guilt of shame

Innocence lost, another youth is gone

With only skittles and a drink

In the summer rain

"On the shoulder of giants" we must revisit

our thoughts. Step by step and revisit their

walks. We can't let this death defeat our efforts even though our life may ever be affected. To the gesture of a mother's kiss

To mourning of our fallen son

No power lies in hate

"Splendor in the grass" rests in the memory

On this young child's face. Tick tock, time passes. A frown face. A clown laughs. Blood to blood, unblemished to the signs of pain

God gives us life, but man takes it in vain.

BEAUTIFUL GRANDDAUGHTERS

FAMILY IS THE BREAD AND BUTTER OF LIFE

IN MEMORY OF THE AUTHOR'S NIECE, PRISCILLA JENKINS

LOVE IS PRICELESS

YOU GOTTA PUT IN THE WORK FOR A GOOD MARRIAGE

IT'S NOT GOING TO BE EASY

NAUTRE'S BEAUTY

Grandparent's rights.

The author hope to use this platform to fight aggressively for grandparents rights. Hopefully, laws will be incorporated to help with this delicate issue.

Delayna

Advertising Page for Businesses

1. Jan'na Healthcare Services

252-212-5941 servicing children's respiratory needs, over 25 years experience

2. Alonda Natural Roots 252-382-3411
3. Saint Stephen's Loving daycare: Your Child is the Heart of Our Business! 252-885-6249
4. Car Mania located 2976 S. Church Street, Rocky Mount NC
They will take the hassle out of purchasing a car.
Call: 252-382-0427
5. Crystal Dickens (owner) of Eye Candy Kouture Hair and Day Spa! Located inside Nukreation Beauty

Mall 413 Mills Rocky Mount NC, 27804 contact: 252-252-907-3704

6. Flat Rate Taxes: Tawanda Harris and Shaunika Evans They are Certified Tax Preparers; they do Taxes for Less. Located @ 101 Triangle Court Suite 4 Nashville, NC 27856 Phone: 252-459-8297

---

7. Electric Image Band located in Rocky Mount NC 252-883-3122

8. Vernon: The Clothes Doctor

   Call: 252-469-9666

   He tailors clothes to fix you

Drica Bellany Blessing Assurance Childcare   252-969-062

Continuation of advertising page

Check Out: Emma's Outstanding Creation for creative hair styling

She is located 4655 Faith Baptist Church Road, Pinetop, NC 27864

Emma is the author's beautician

For home cook food, check out **Tray-Seas Soul Food!** Located 306 S. Maine St. Princeville, NC no. 252-698-2191

CEO: Tracey Bridgers

Also, check out: **The Kids Place** located on 425 Hammond St. Rocky Mount NC contact: 252-977-1778 Their mission is to provide a safe haven for children

Victory Learning Academy Daycare

620 Grace street Rocky Mount NC

Owner: Kristina Simpson 252-446-7154

A " home away from home"

Little Angeles Daycare located 108

Timberlane Drive Rocky Mount NC

Contact No. 252-985-730

The owner pride herself in providing a healthy atomspher for children to grow and learn.

Real Estate

Tyneesha Palmer Realtor will help you find a home that will fix your needs.

Contact: 1-919- 593-0481,

She has worked with the best agents.

Joletha Coley: Owner of Four Seasons Beauty Salon 531 Albemarle Ave. Rocky Mount NC, 27801 Great Beautician! For transportation needs, check out Chase Lanier: Sale Consultant @ Univerity Ford Contact: 1-984-789 images

https://stock.adobe.com/search/free?filters%5Bcontent_type%3Aphoto%5D=1&filters%5Bcontent_type%3Aillustration%5D=1&filters%5Bcontent_type%3Azip_vector%5D=1&filters%5Bcontent_type%3Avideo%5D=0&filters%5Bcontent_type%3Atemplate%5D=0&filters%5Bcontent_type%3A3d%5D=0&filters%5Bcontent_type%3Aaudio%5D=0&filters%5Binclude_stock_enterprise%5D=0&filters%5Bis_editorial%5D=0&filters%5Bfree_coll

ection%5D=1&filters%5Bcontent_type%3Ai
mage%5D=1&k=scenery+illustration&order
=relevance&safe_search=1&limit=100&searc
h_page=6&search_type=pagination&get_face
ts=0&asset_id=286743675

https://stock.adobe.com/images/aurora-
borealis-landscape-northern-lights-with-stars-
snowdrifts-and-fir-tree-night-winter-snowy-
background-vector-illustration/374691092

mages.search.yahoo.com/search/images;_ylt=
AwrE19BLV_1hXDcAPTVXNyoA;_ylu=Y2
9sbwNiZjEEcG9zAzEEdnRpZANMT0NVS
TAxOF8xBHNlYwNzYw--
?p=free+royalty+free+pictures+of+black+an
d+white+children+playing+together&fr=tigh
tropetb

**https://www.istockphoto.com/pho
tos/black-empowerment**

https://www.istockphoto.com/photos/black-man-praying

The author would like to thank:

Kimberly Hill for her help proofing Priscilla Smile Two. Also, the poets: Jamey Wilkins, Gidget Seaborne, Erica Davis, Lillian Jenkins, Geraldine Jenkins, Earnest Jenkins, Brittany Hill and Matthew J. Jenkins for their poems and pieces of literature. These are all the author's family members.

If you enjoyed reading this book, check out the author's other books: Child Speak Out!, Little Mirror and The Bronze Plantation & Mr. Ed

The author hopes you enjoy reading these collection of poems.

Special Shout out to my oldest sister, Gidget Seaborne

At an early age, Gidget had a vision. She decided she didn't want to be one of the have nots. So she worked hard to improve her situation, she looked around and saw people struggling and this motivated her to study harder.

Her life's journey began when she worked as a CNA. She discovered her passion which was helping people in delicate situations. Eventually, she decided to go back to school. She advanced her education and became a LPN. And with meticulous planning, she finally became a RN. Gidget worked steadfast to achieve her dream. She worked 44 years in the nursing field until she retired.

My sister has always been my inspiration. After seeing what she had accomplished, it motivated me to reach out and grab my opportunities before it demised before my eyes. Over the years I premeditated and tried my best to imitate her. My sister didn't let a flawed system stop her.

Dreams don't come to you. You gotta put in work. Also, I would like to thank my baby sister, Lillian Jenkins, even though, she is the youngest, her wisdom has helped me grow as a person. I thank God for her.

Additionally, I would like to thank my brother, Earnest Jenkins. He forged a way from out of dust to become a force of reckoning; he became a Captain in the United States Army.

My loving parents, Eddie and Odell Jenkins was my foundation along with my uncle and aunt, Carrie and Jack Harrison. Also, my cousin, Bettie Harrisson, she pushed me beyond my comfort zone to perfect my craft. That's what motivates me to push on, that's what keeps me strong.

Now, enjoy the beauty!

stockphoto.com/search/2/image?phrase=bla

ck+and+white+landscape...

He Smiled

He smiled, but I was so busy thinking of my negative experiences. I needed a new car, home, and money. Then, on my daily walk, I heard a whisp from the wind. He spoke to me kindly, now, I am scared, so I started to run. Oh, it could not be him. Then, I started laughing out loud. After a long exhausting day, I laid down. I closed my eyes soaking in my daily experiences. Then, I heard a voice, yes, I been with you my child from conception to your present day dilemmas. I was in the path in the wilderness that led you back into your mother's arms. I was the one who closed the venomous snake's mouth when you interrupted him feasting on a rat. It was me who eased your pain in a moment of weakness, after a near death experience when you lost control of your car. I lifted you out of the face of danger. Then, your car exploded, people wondered how you survived.
I, Jehovah God have been walking beside you, but you were so caught up in self pity, you brushed me off like a fly. You were blinded by materialistic things, too busy to cherish the blessings before your eyes. But, I can see past the facade, I, Jehovah can read the heart. I knew one day my child, you will see all the beauty that is surmounting, that's what I been waiting on, and that's what makes me smile. It's God's Grace that allows you to revisit history and allow you to appreciate your blessings. Now you give praise allowing my teachings to consume your heart. The reason you are here today, is no accident. It's because of my grace and mercy.

Look and see the beauty!

Priscilla's Smile

In that moment, in that hour, in that minute
and in that second
All troubles ceased

Butterflies surrounded Priscilla.
Then, I remembered my mother's words
Keep the faith, my child
Faith will keep you
Grace will empower you
Hope will substain you
My love will protect you
Let the Bible guide you
Love you

Then I closed my eyes
Oh, was it just yesterday when Priscilla was a little girl, laughing and playing with that beautiful smile?

www.ingramcontent.com/pod-product-compliance
Lightning Source LLC
Chambersburg PA
CBHW020421010526
44118CB00010B/354